# Color My Deen

An Islamic-Themed Coloring Book
25 Original Designs

by Fatima Padela

Copyright © 2021 by Fatima Padela

www.fatimapadeladesigns.com
Instagram @fatima.padela.designs
Facebook @fatima.padela.designs

All rights reserved. No part of this publication may be reproduced, distributed or transmitted in any form or by any means, including photocopying, recording or other electronic or mechanical methods, without the prior written permission of the owner, except as permitted by U.S. copyright law.

ISBN: 978-1-7367785-0-0

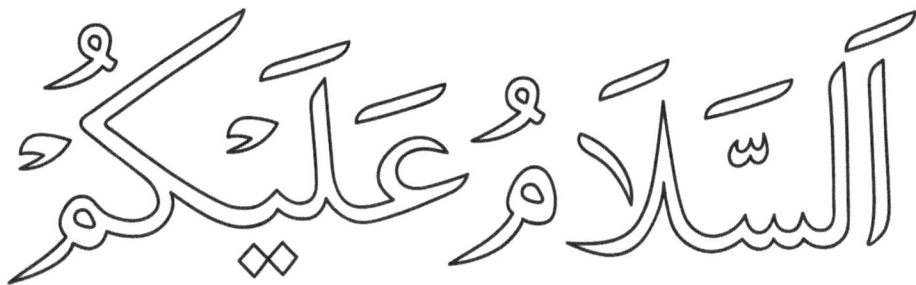

(Peace Be Upon You)

Assalamu'alaikum,

Inside this Islamic-themed coloring book you will find 25 original works of art.

The pages are designed to fit in a standard 8"x10" frame.

I'm truly grateful you have chosen to spend your time here and hope you find it relaxing and peaceful!

Sincerely,

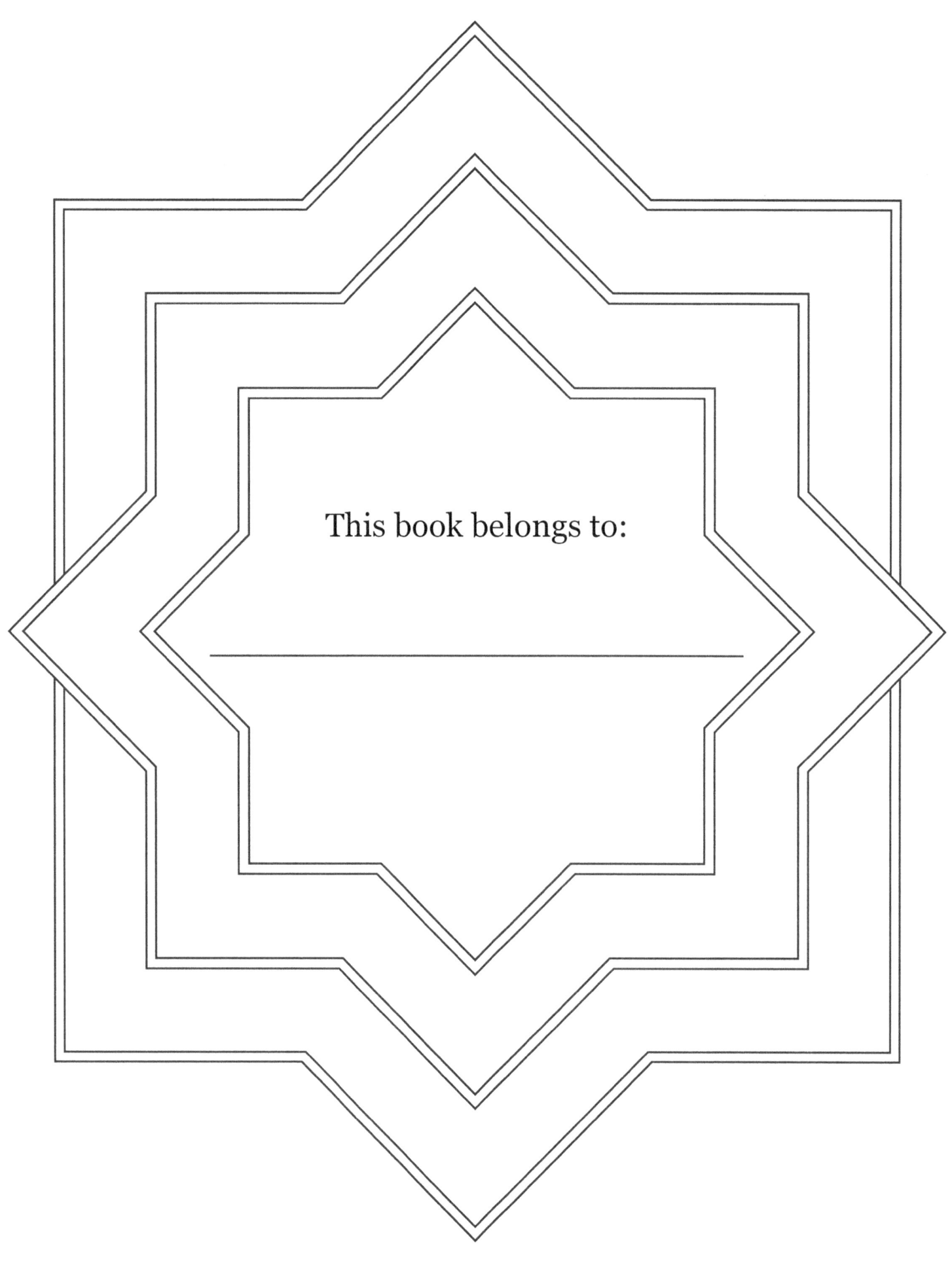
This book belongs to:

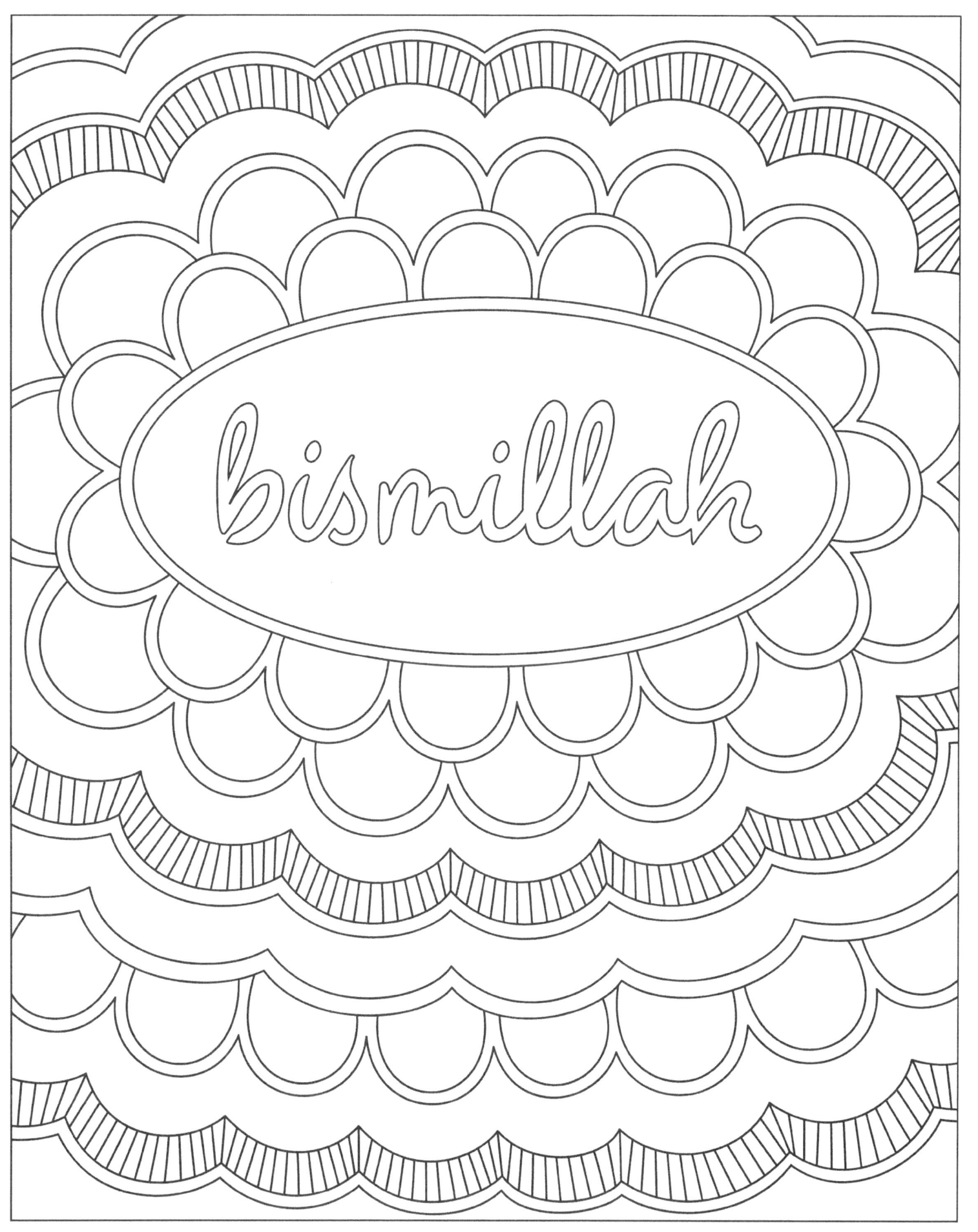

fatima padela designs

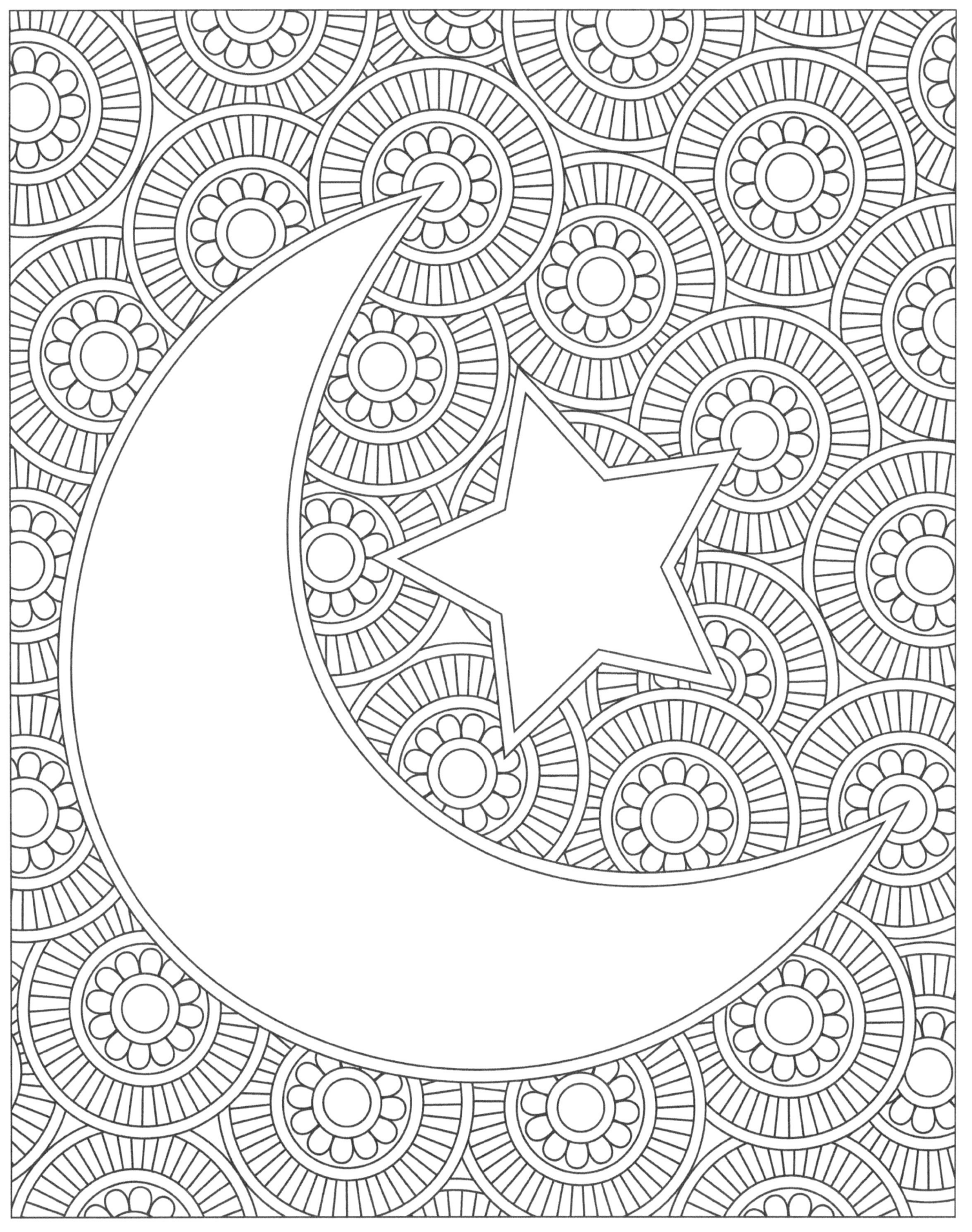

fatima padela designs

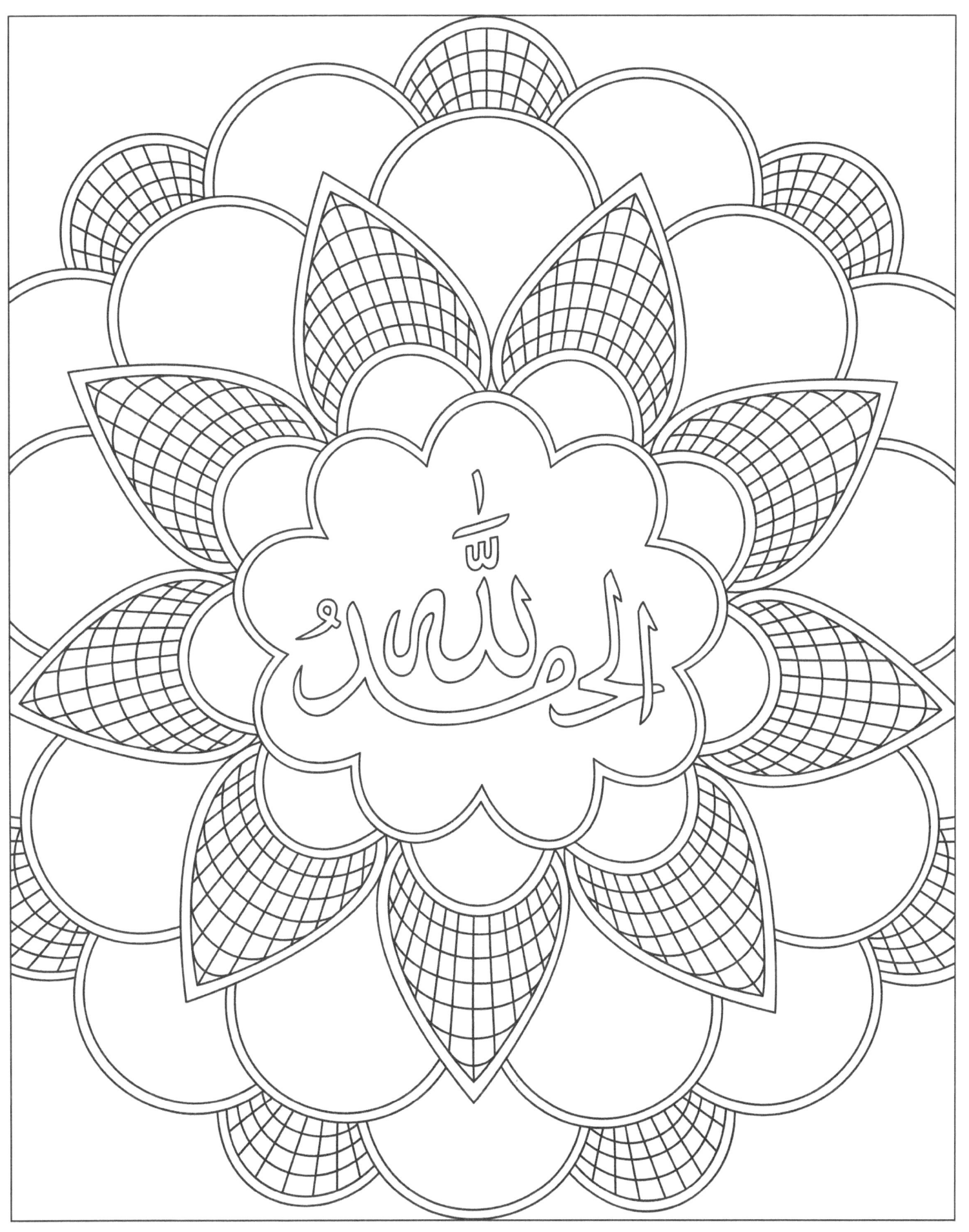

fatima padela designs

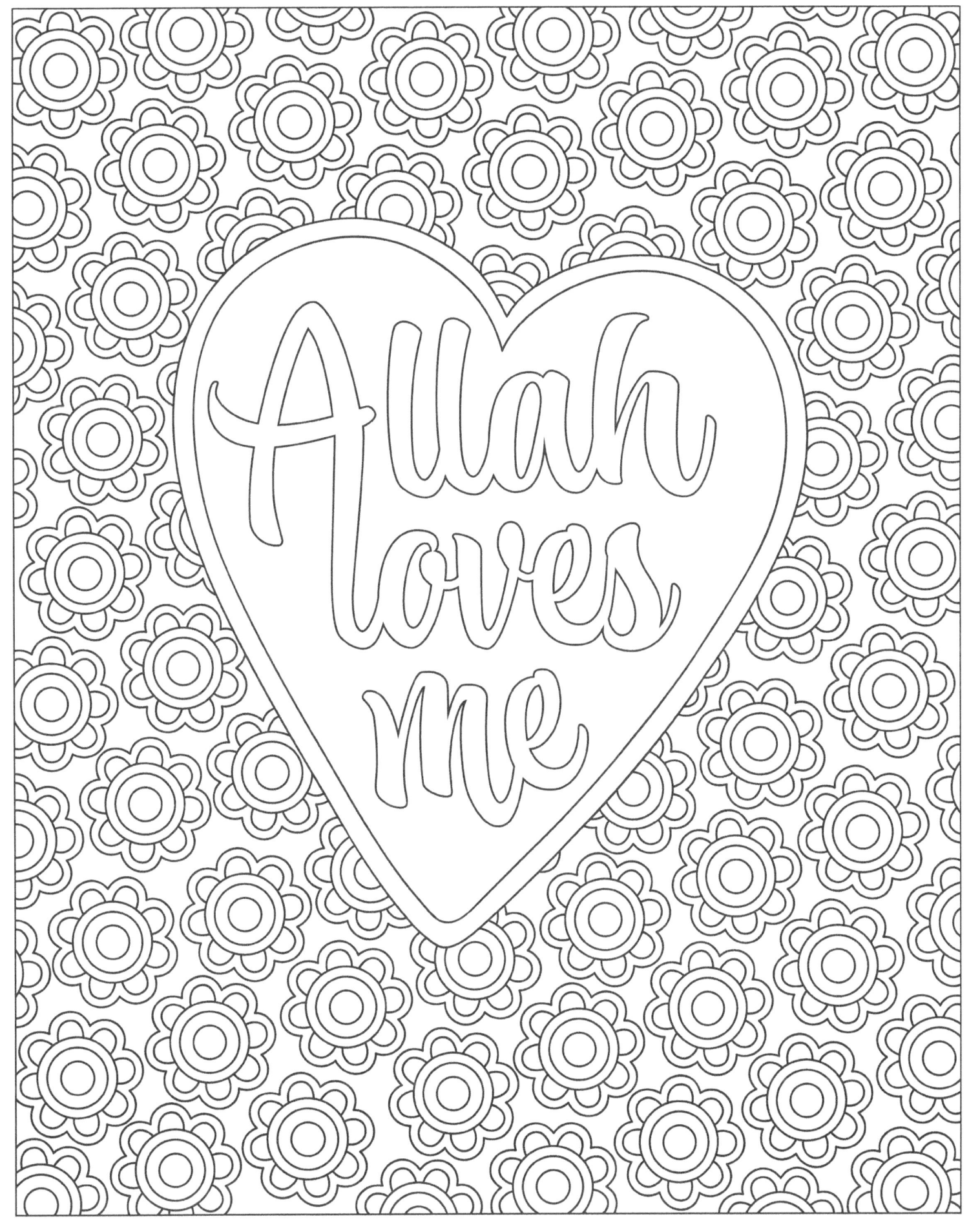

fatima padela designs

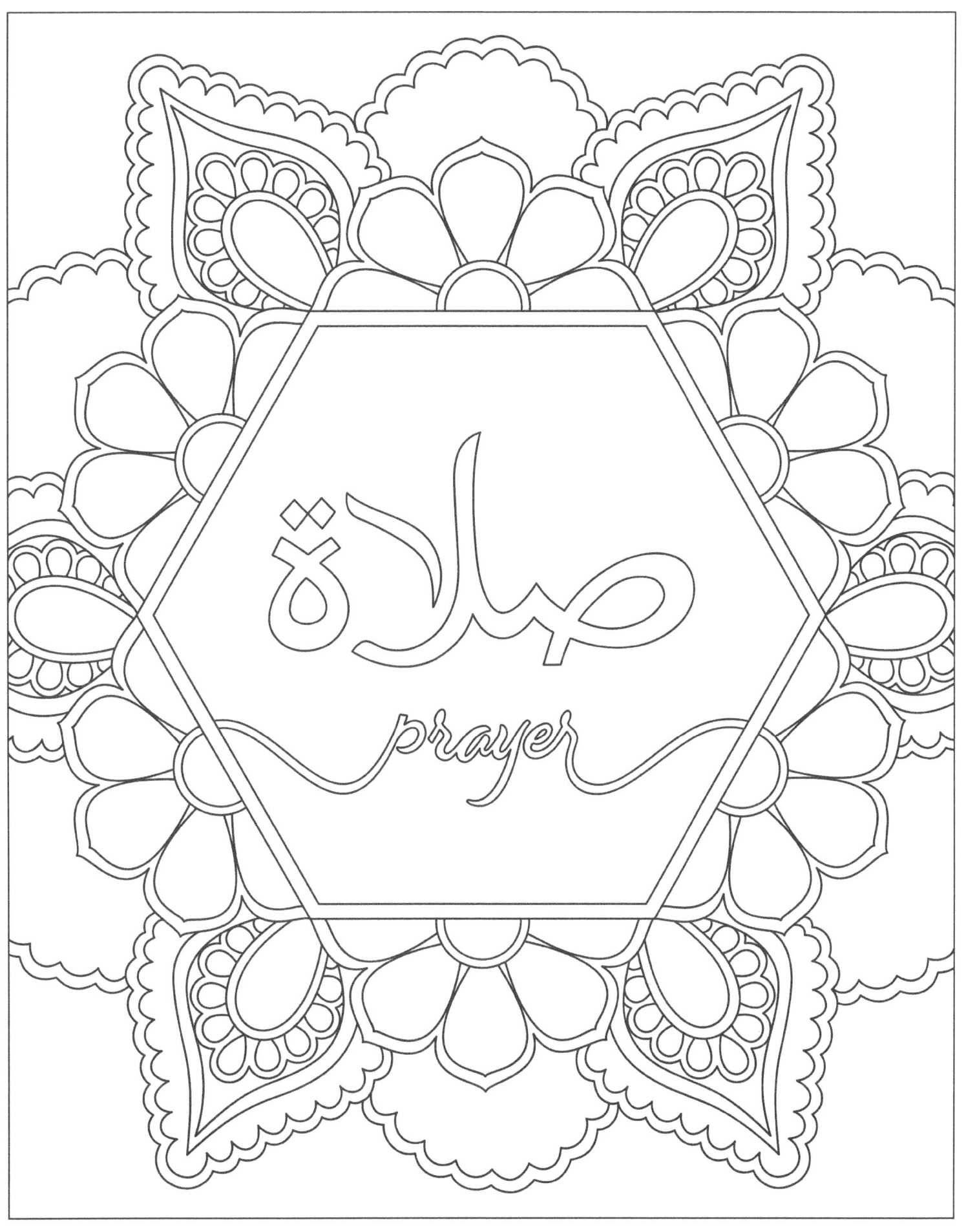

fatima padela designs

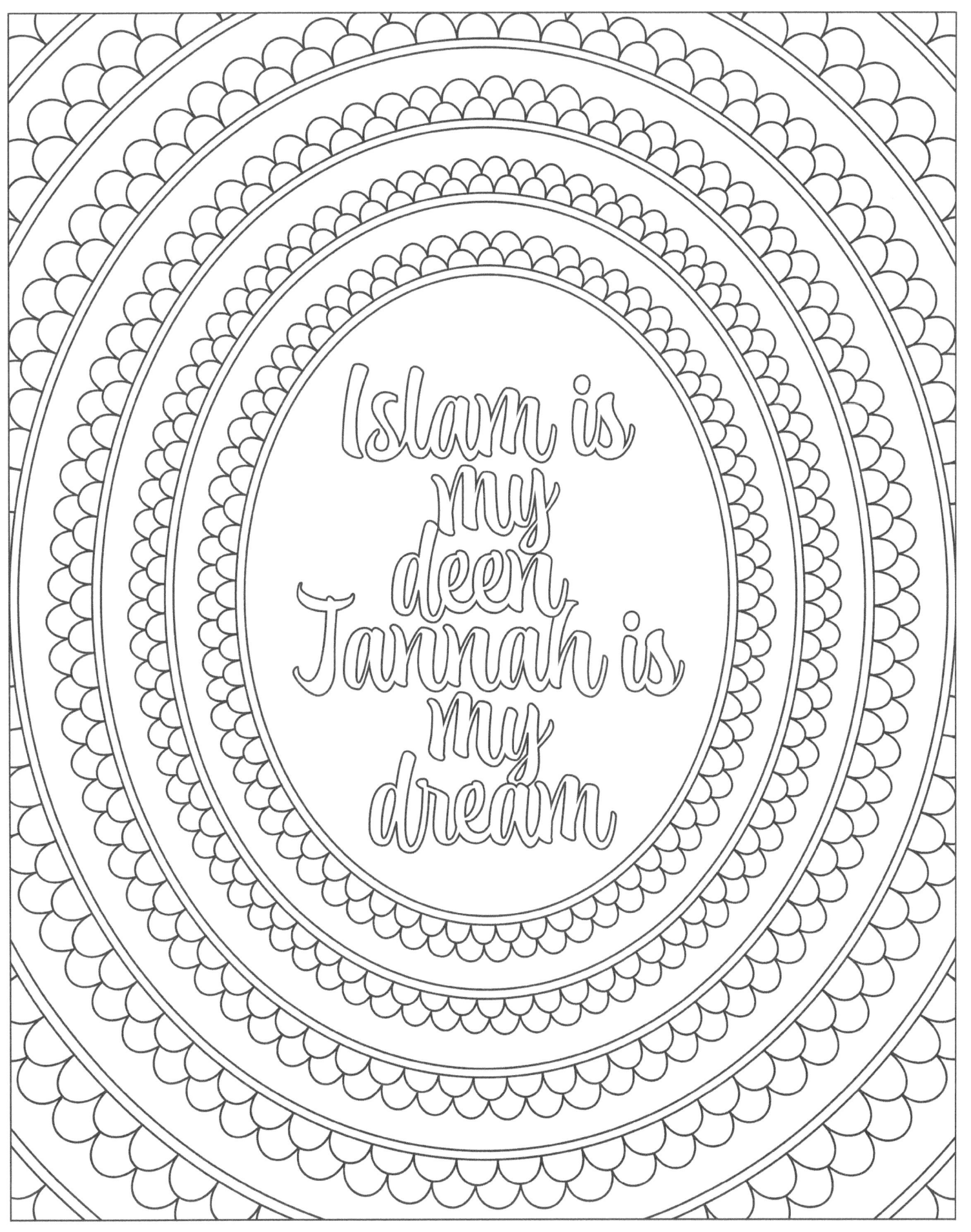

fatima padela designs

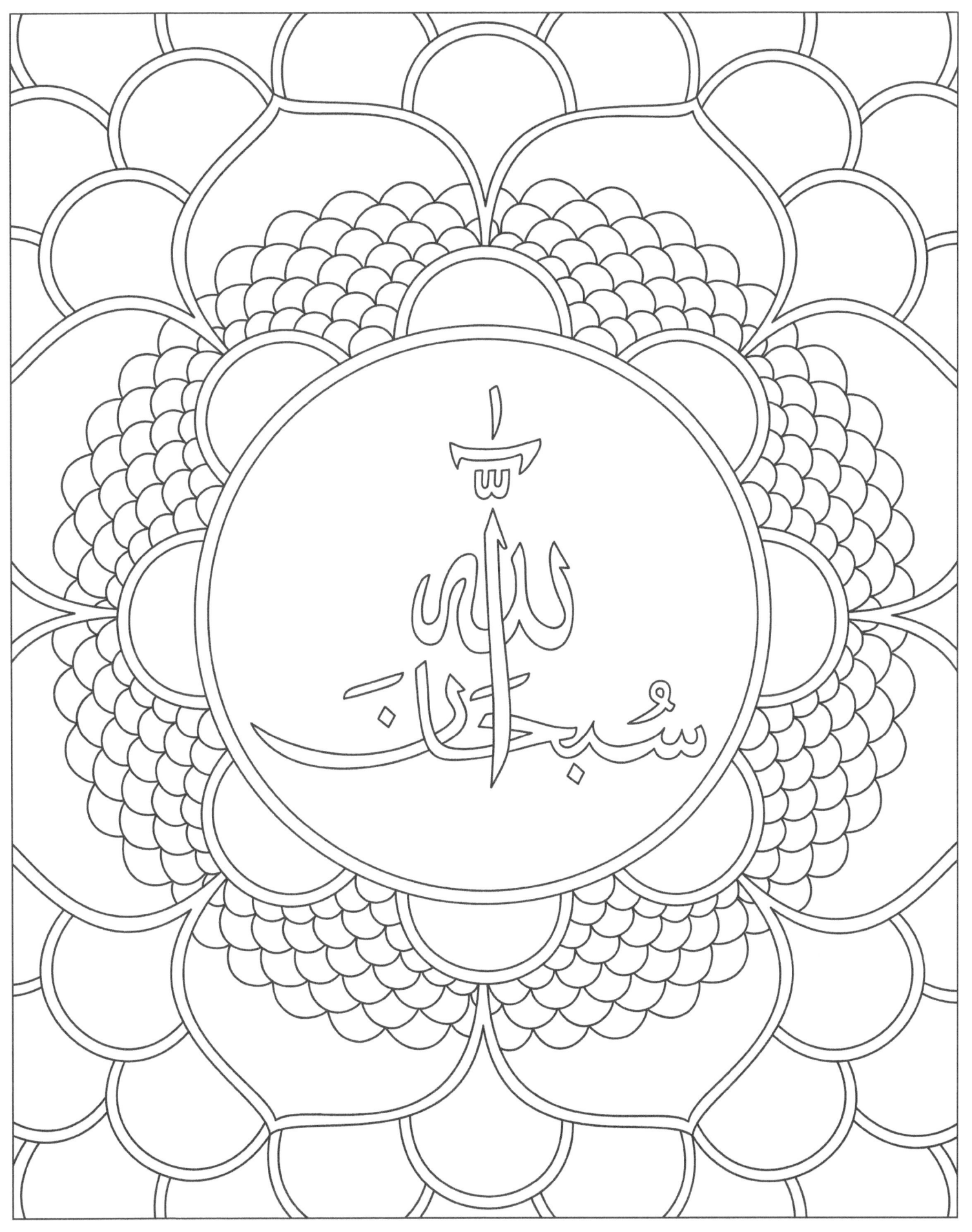

fatima padela designs

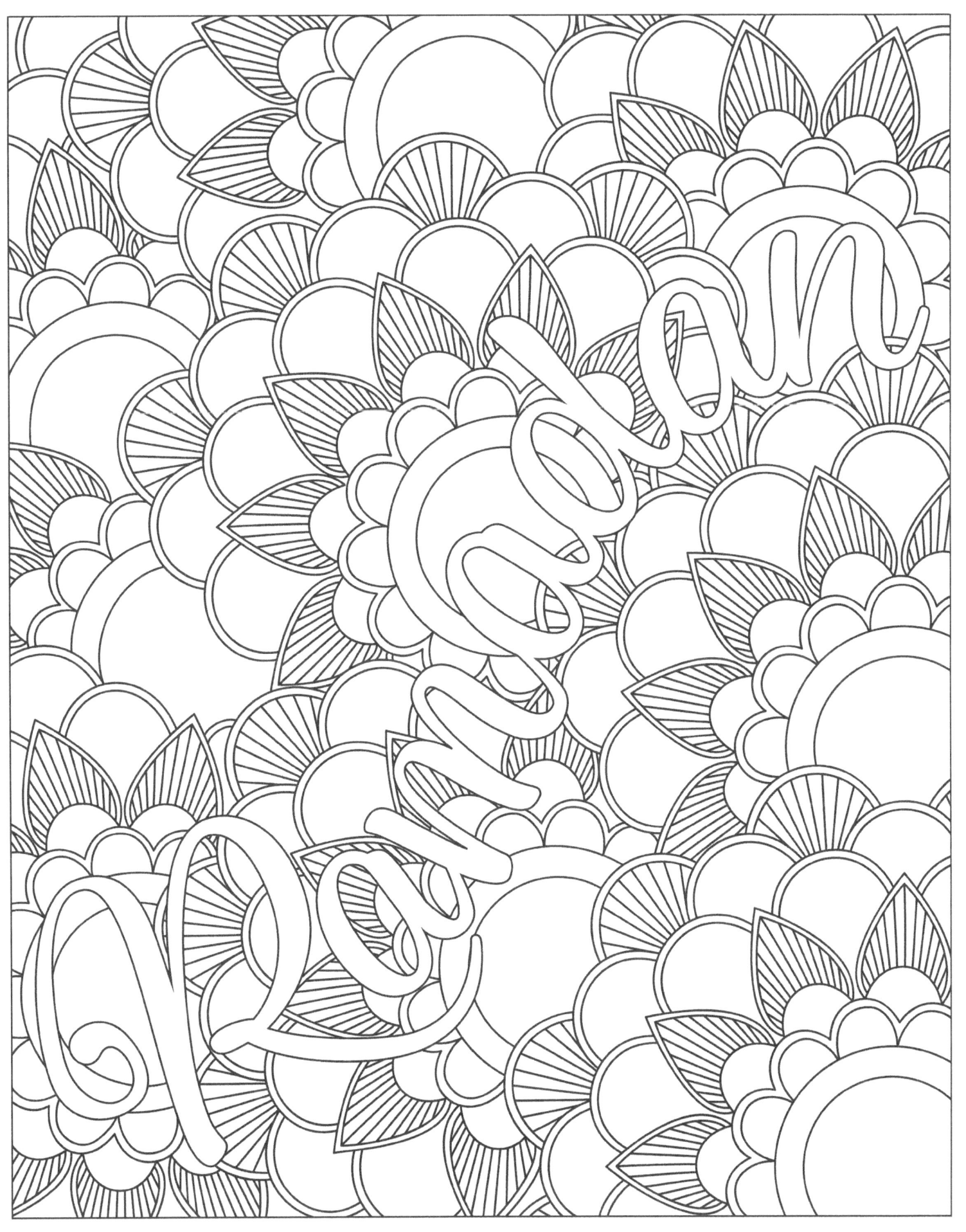

fatima padela designs

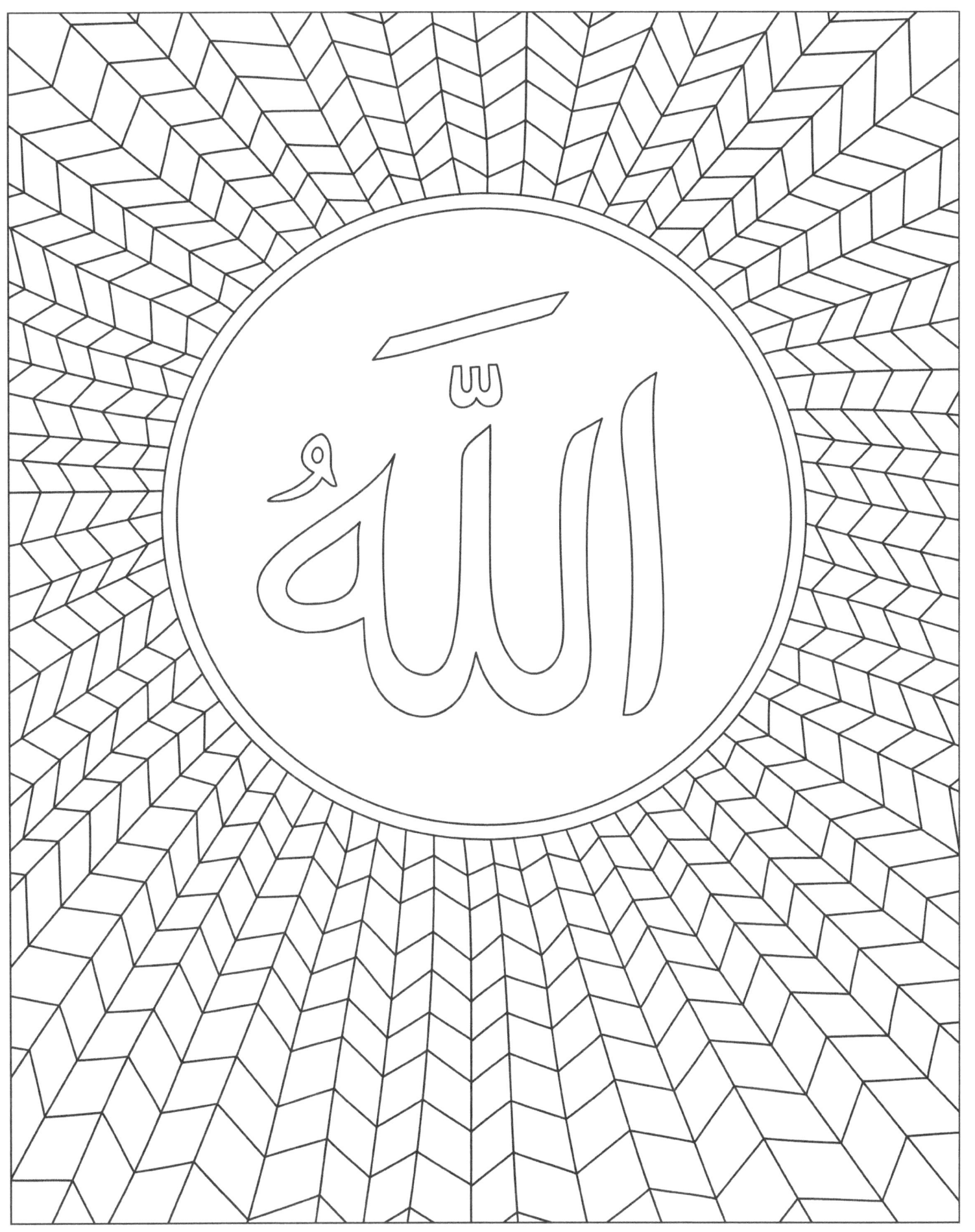

fatima padela designs

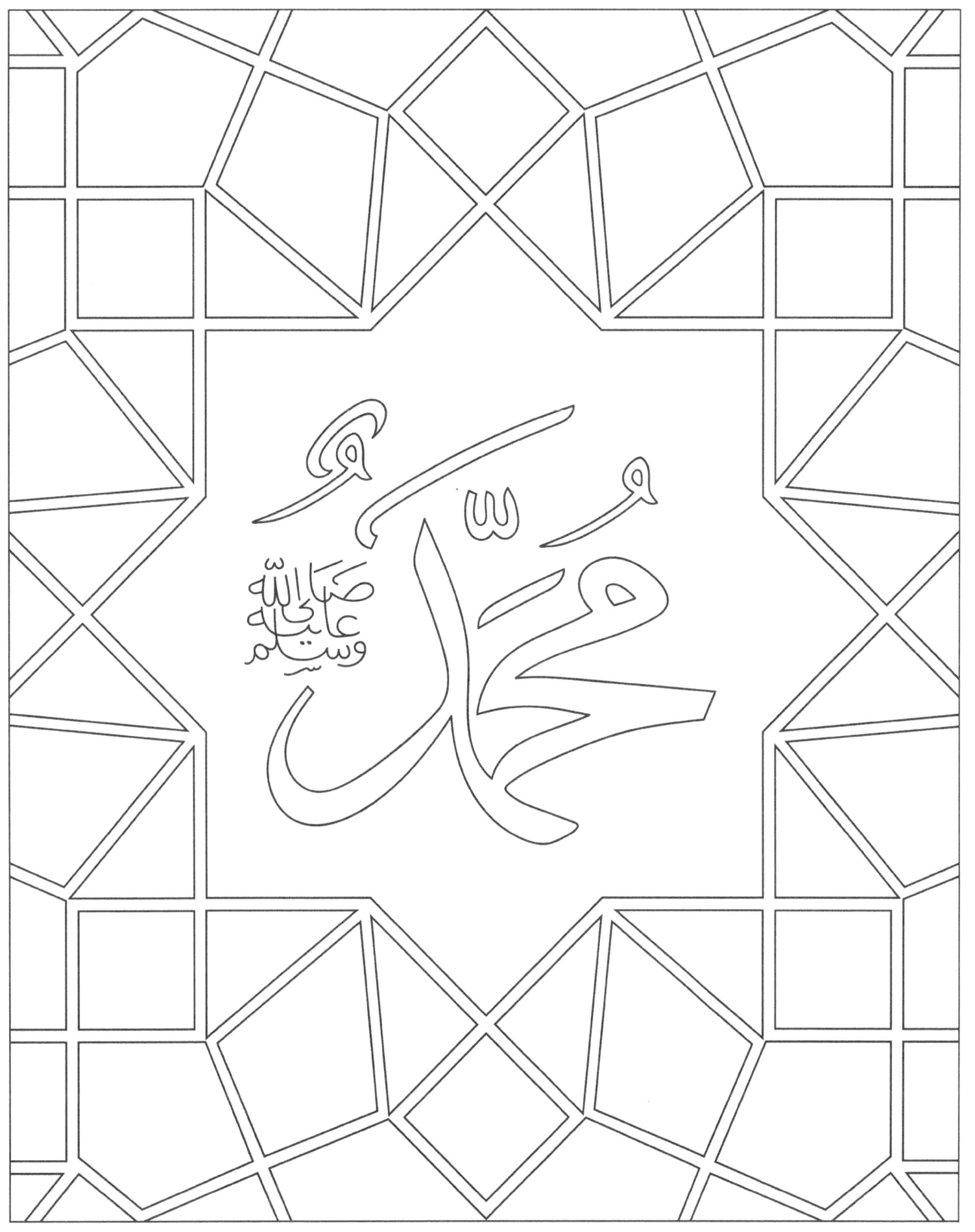

fatima padela designs

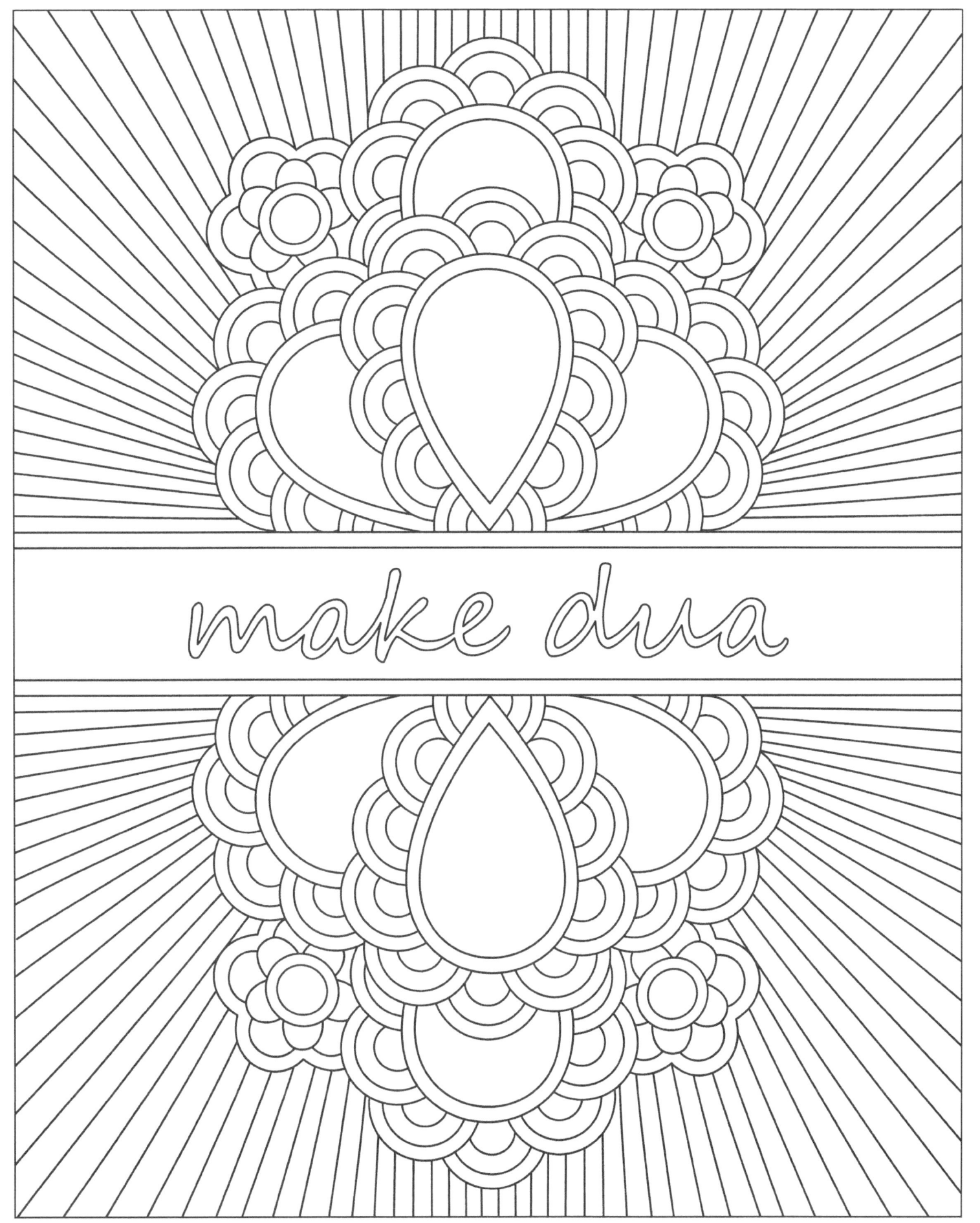

fatima padela designs

fatima padela designs

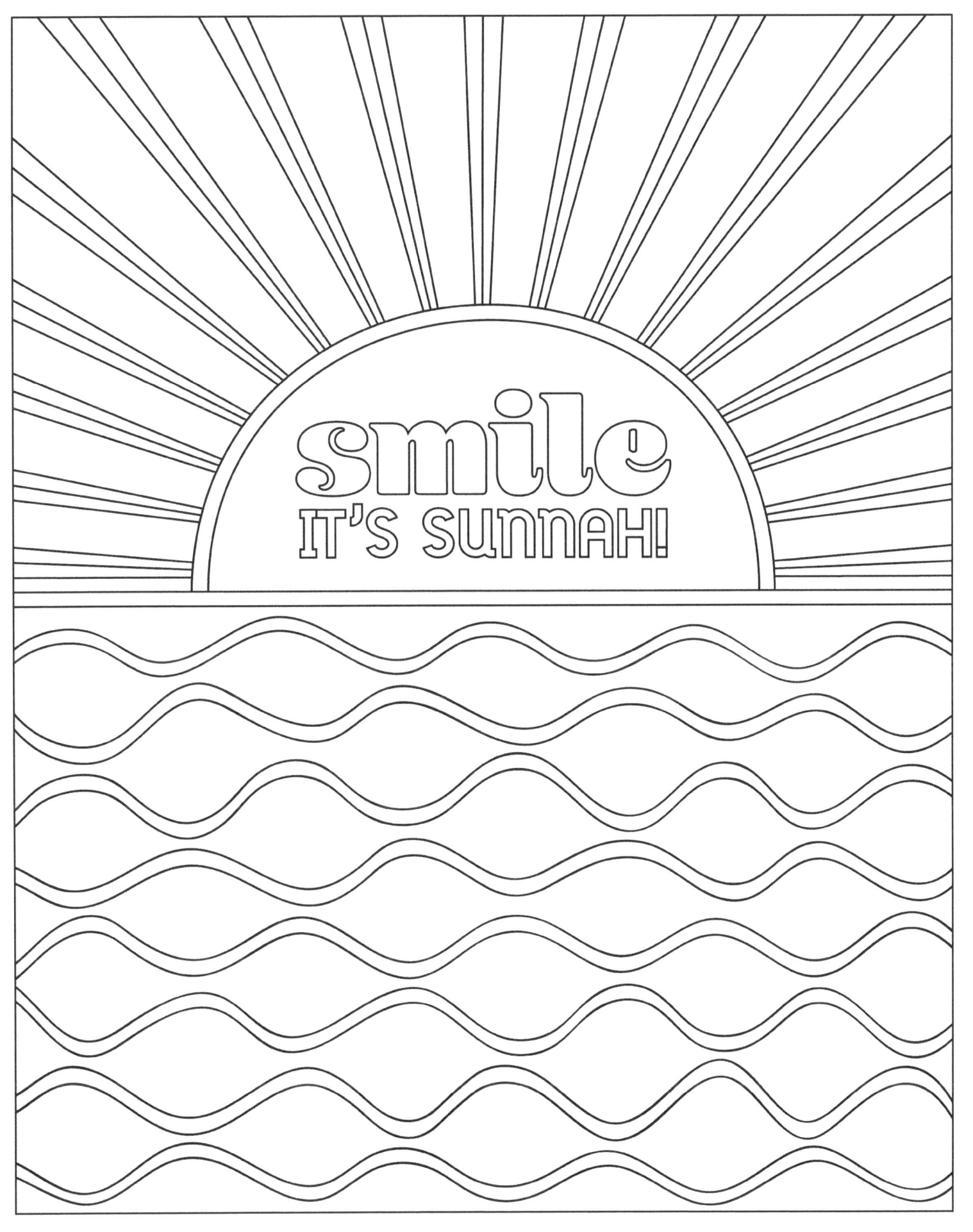

fatima padela designs

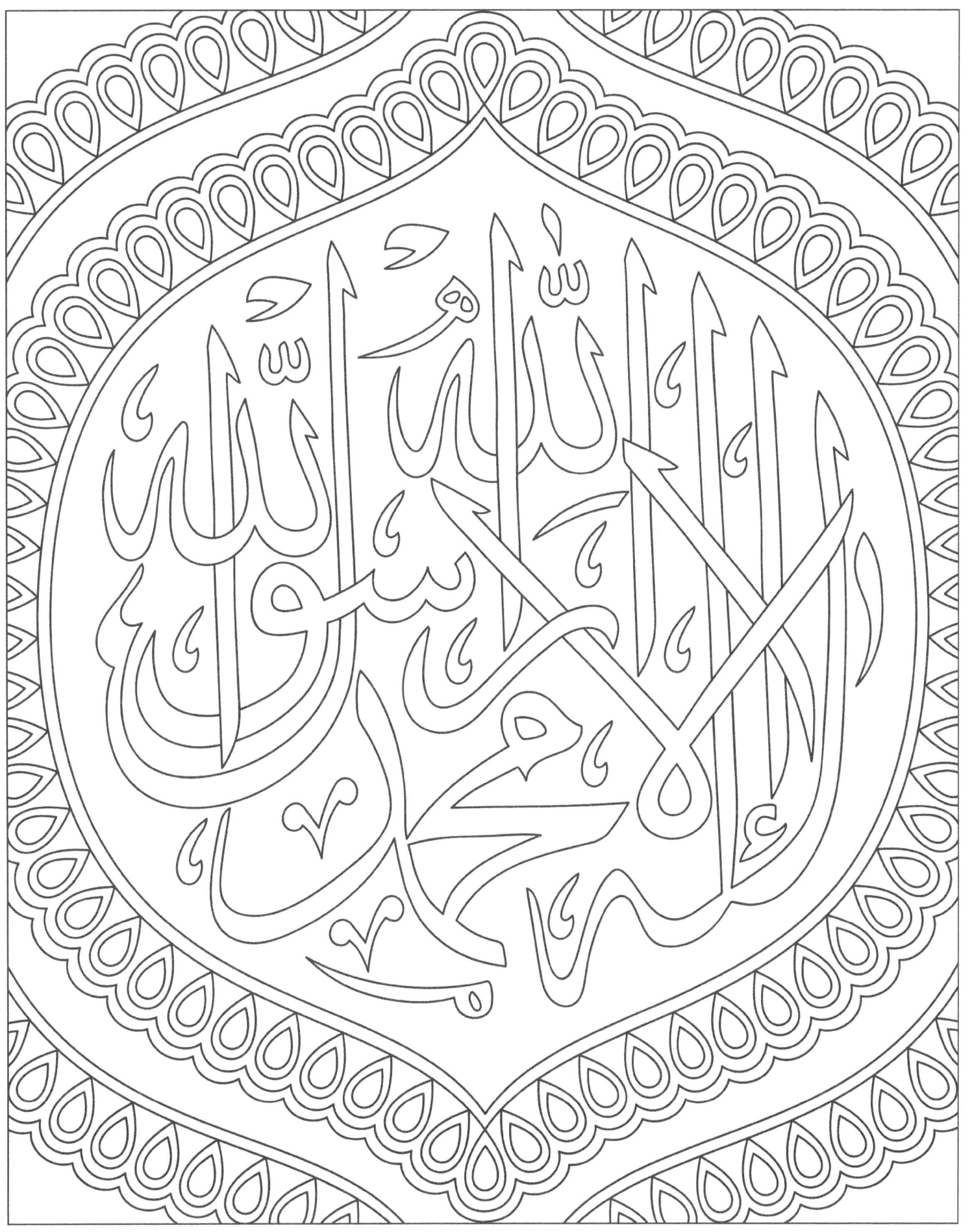

fatima padela designs

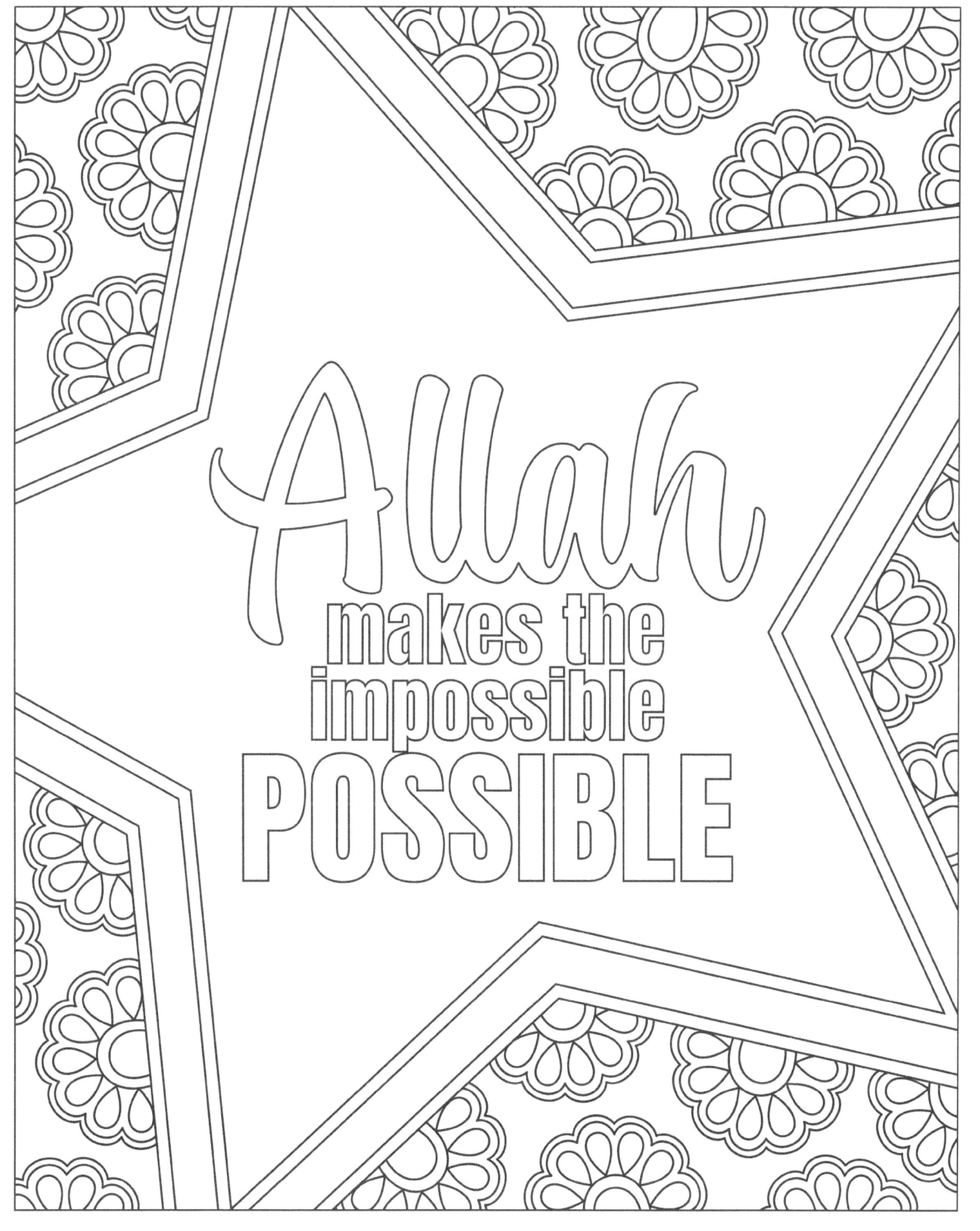

fatima padela designs

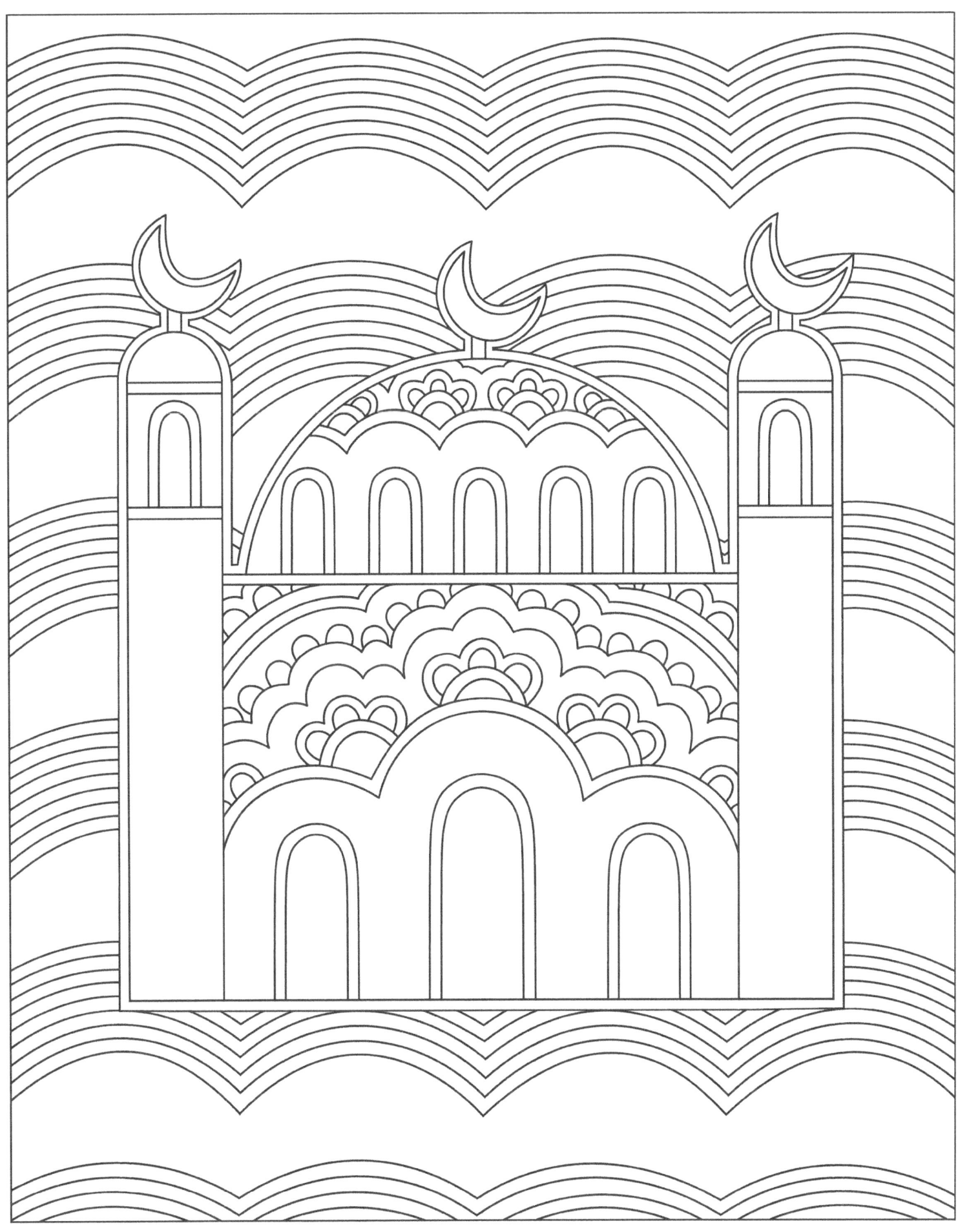

fatima padela designs

fatima padela designs

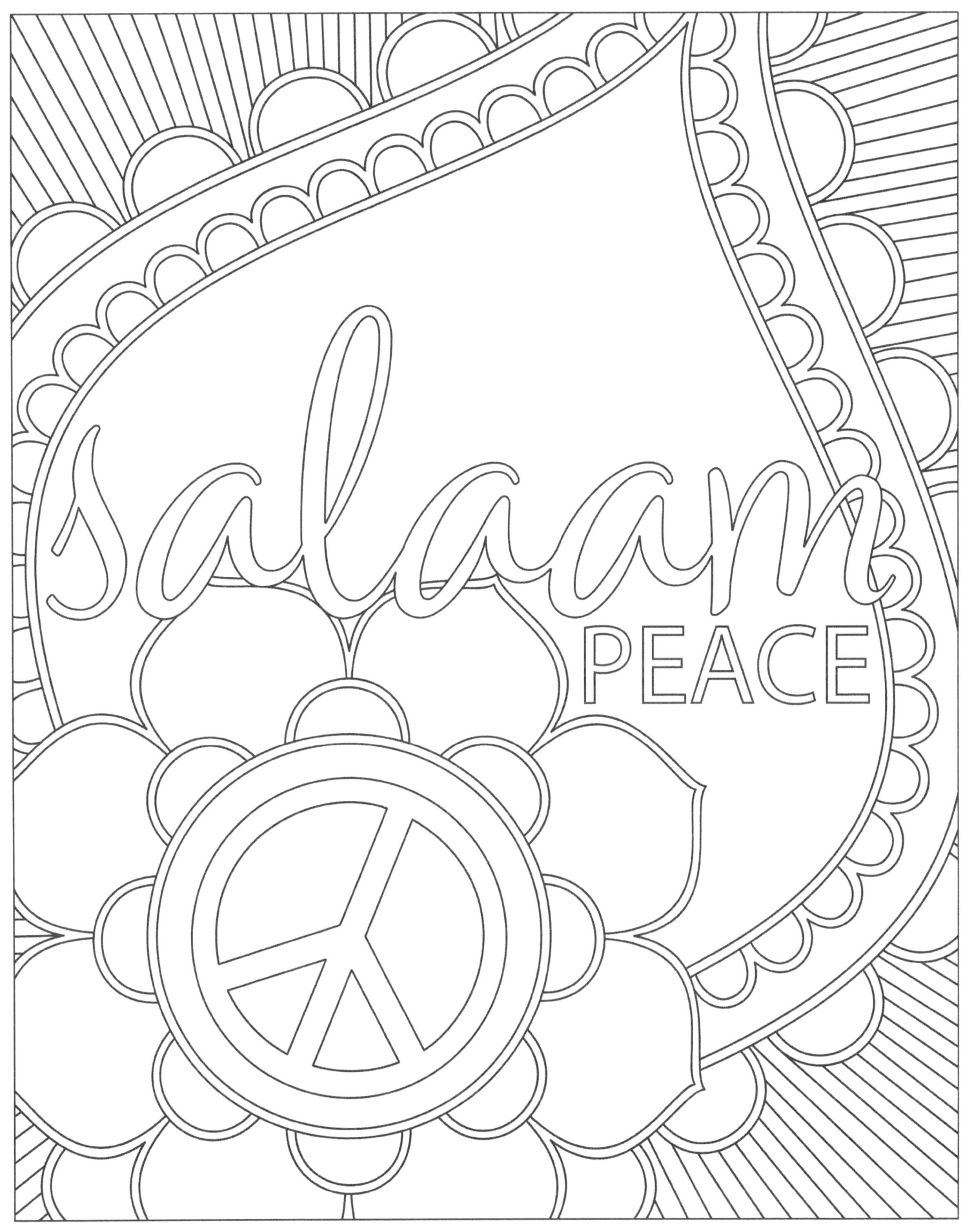

fatima padela designs

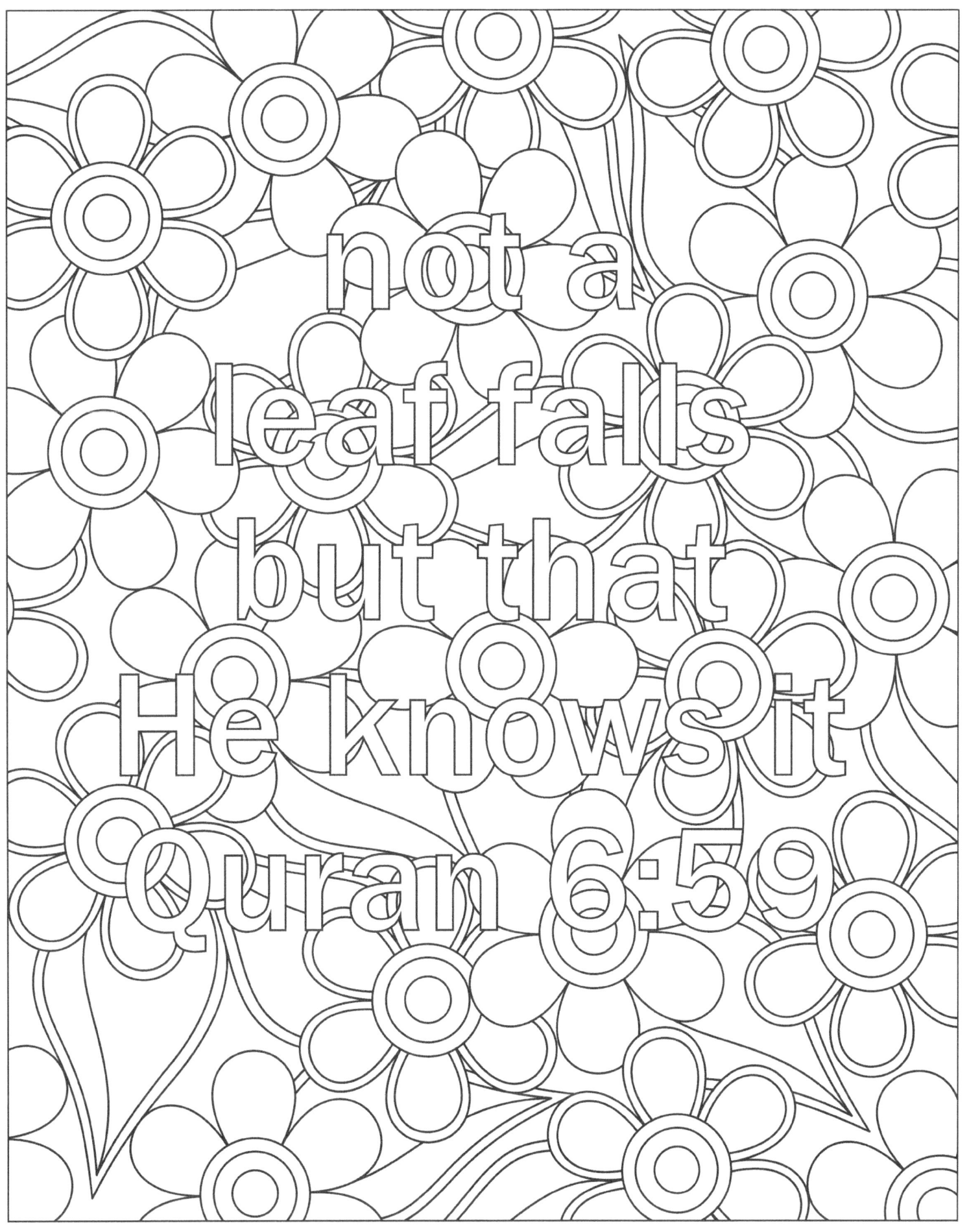

fatima padela designs

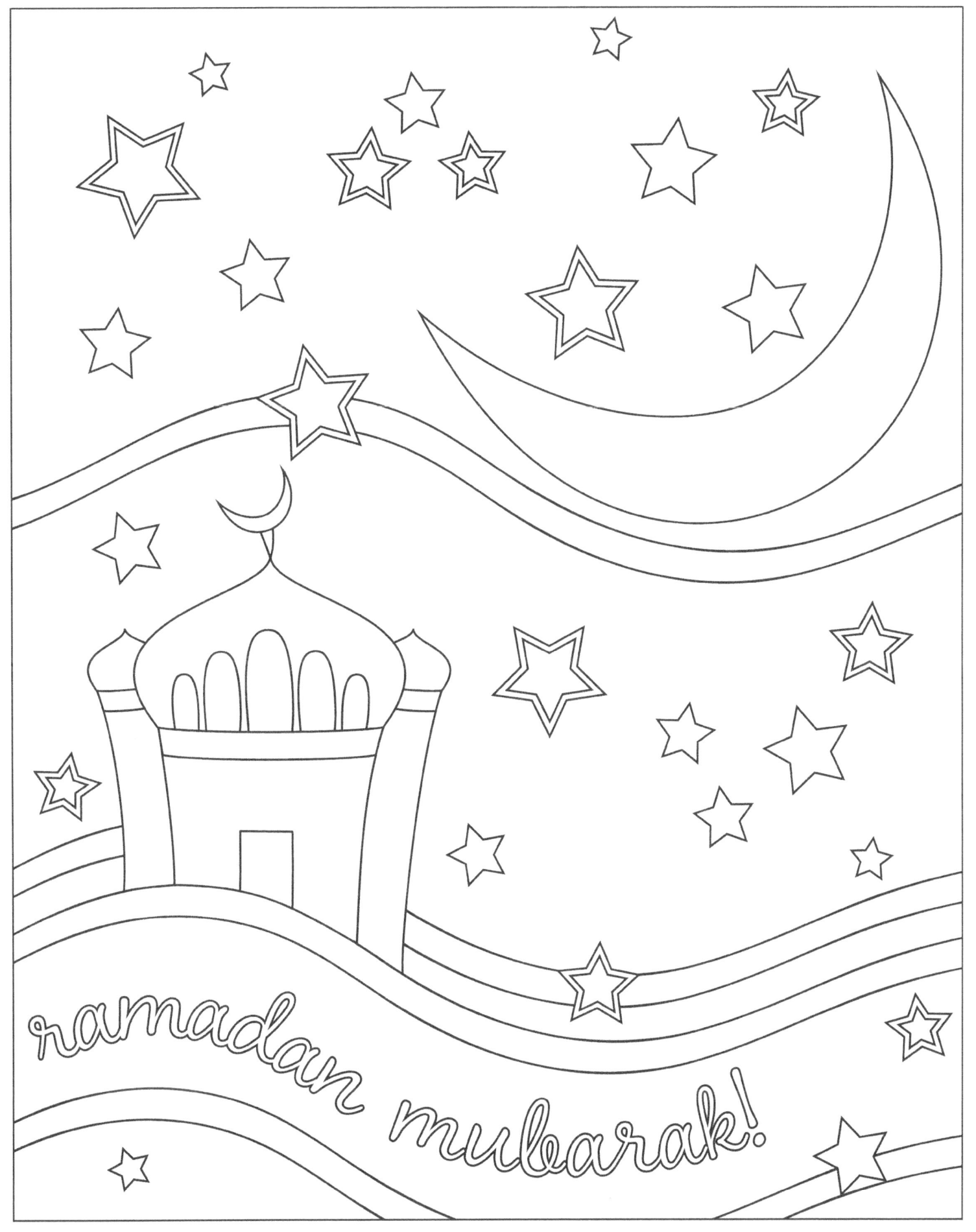

fatima padela designs

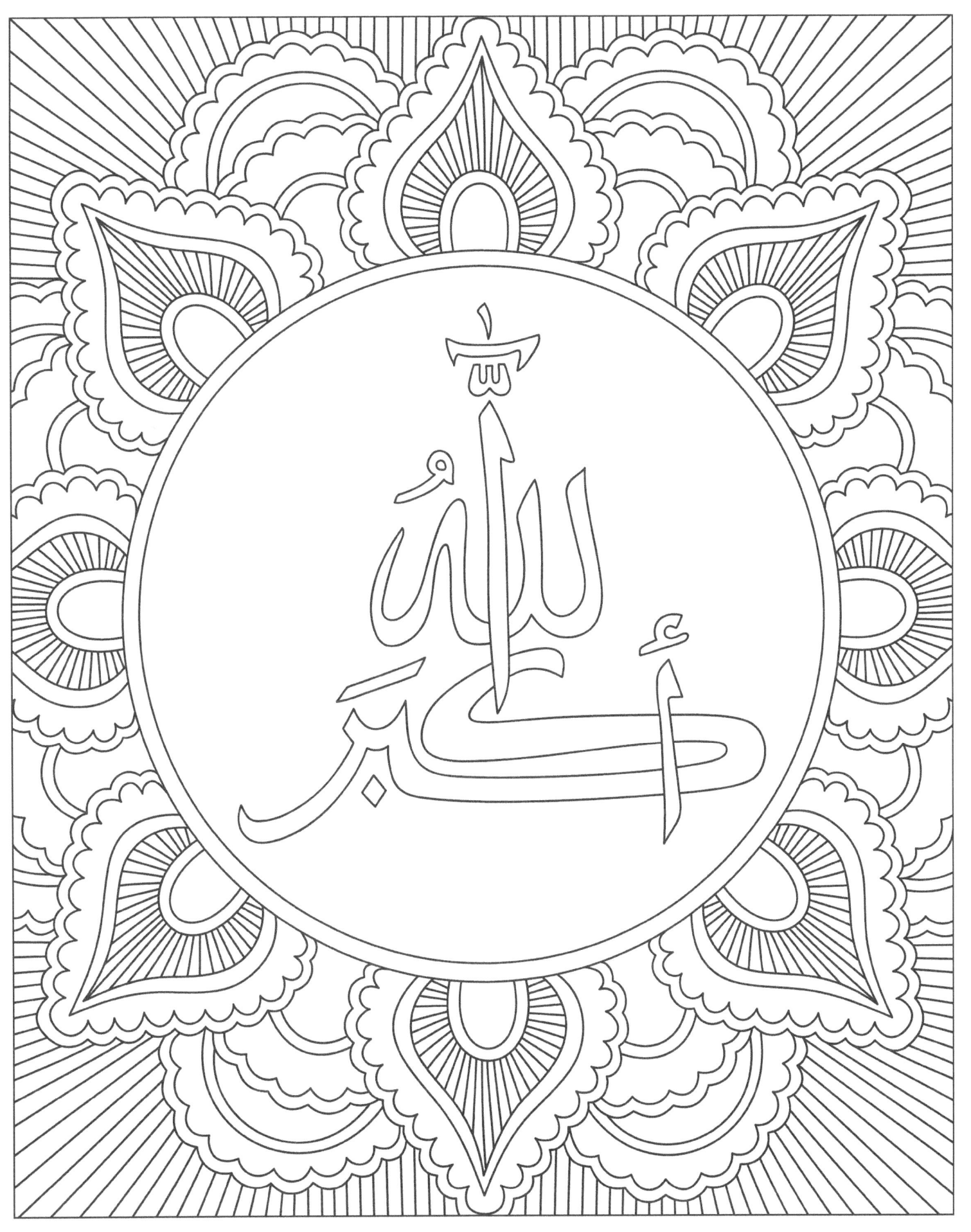

fatima padela designs

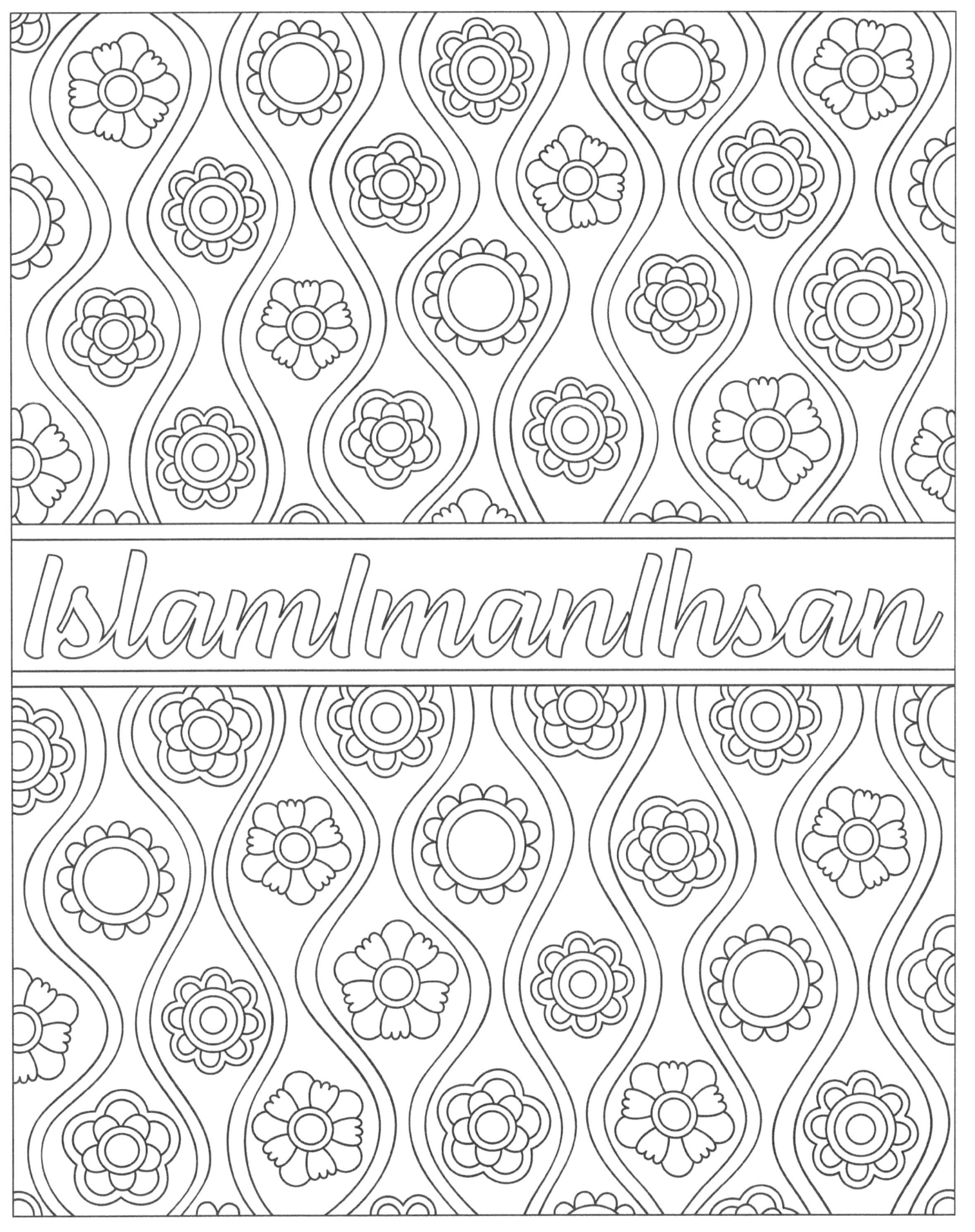

fatima padela designs

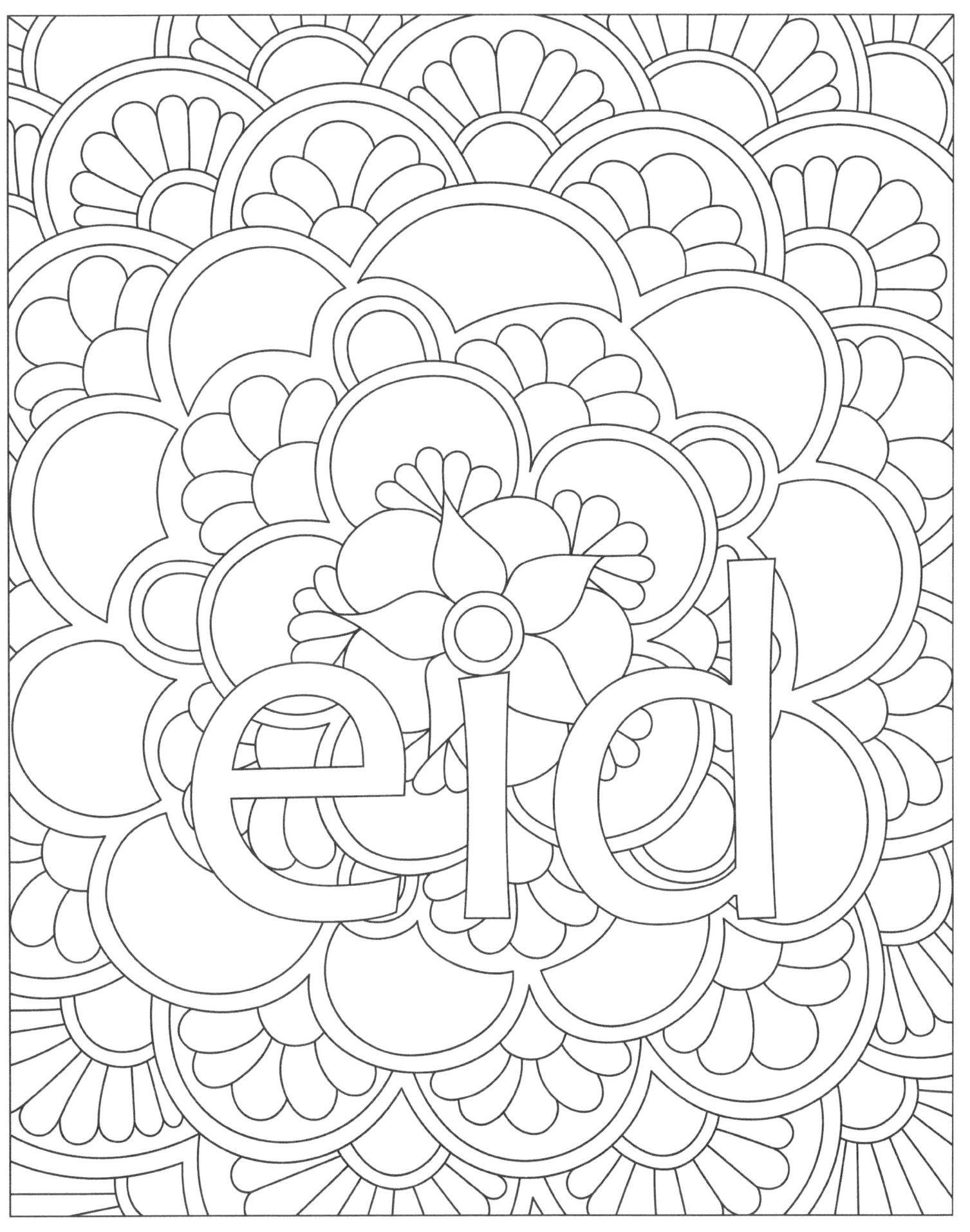

fatima padela designs

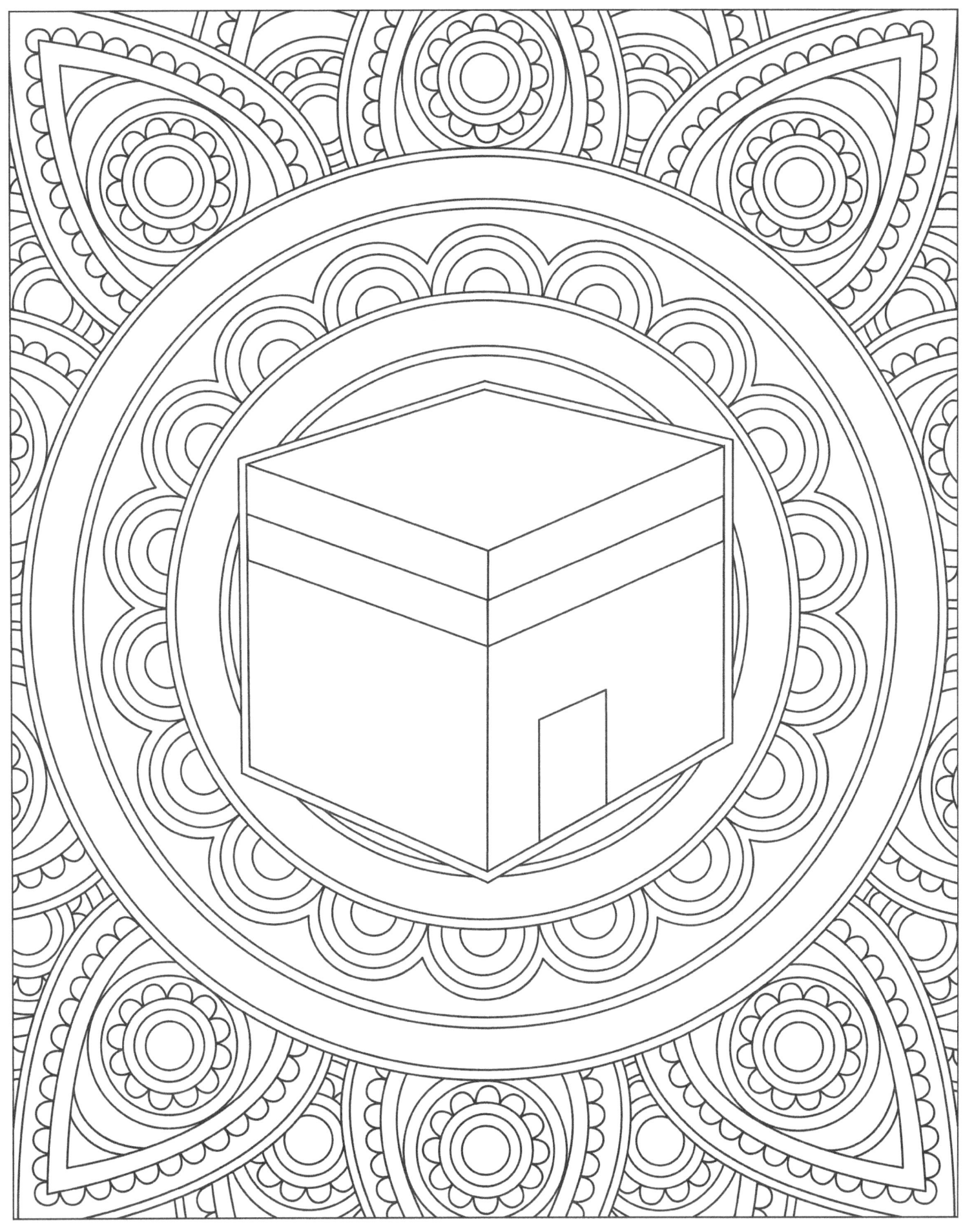

fatima padela designs

fatima padela designs